T0157168

MASTER OF MY
Destiny

Whatever your race, skin color, nationality or circumstances, whether born privileged or not, your ability to succeed, lies squarely within.

TINUKE FAWOLE

author HOUSE®

AuthorHouse™
1663 Liberty Drive
Bloomington, IN 47403
www.authorhouse.com
Phone: 1-800-839-8640

First published by AuthorHouse   11/21/2011

ISBN: 978-1-4670-6987-8 (sc)
ISBN: 978-1-4670-6985-4 (ebk)

Library of Congress Control Number: 2011918883

Printed in the United States of America

CONTENTS

DEDICATION

This Book Is Dedicated To:

My Loving Savior and Lord, Jesus Christ:
My source, my strength, my sustainer, my
all-in-all.

My darling husband, Alaba:
You inspire me, motivate me and cheer me on,
to always do my best.

My beloved parents, Elder & Mrs. Enoch and
Sabainah Dare:
You prepared me, guided me and continue to
inspire me.

My wonderful children, Fiyin, Ope, Gbolu and
Damisi:
You give me joy and peace every day. You
bring a smile to my face always.

My dear and courageous sister, Bola:
Thank you for your heroic sacrifice and
precious gift to me.

ACKNOWLEDGEMENTS

With Special Thanks:

To Mr. Paul Parks, Dr. & Mrs. Dayo and Dapo Falase, Dr. Yemi Badero and Mr. Daniel Fawole for willingly sharing their stories.

To Dr. Abi Adegboye, my senior colleague in writing, for her advice, help and guidance all along the way.

To my daughters, Fiyin and Ope for copy editing the text and taking time out of their busy schedules to do so.

To my husband, Alaba, for his moral and financial support, his useful suggestions and contributions and for editing the book. Yeah, he's got hidden talent!

FOREWORD

$\mathfrak{M}$aster of My Destiny is more than a decade
long idea whose time has come and I am so
very proud of my wife for taking the bull by the
horns and staying the arduous course of pulling
this off.

At first thought, my preference would have
been for someone neutral and with impeccable
public reputation to write the preface to this
book. This I thought would negate the perception
of bias and not be misconstrued as blowing
one's horn. But on second thought, I consider it
a great pleasure to do the honors.

All protocols aside, Master of My Destiny is
a masterpiece. The contents are well thought
out and crafted for easy reading. It is a grand
product of solid legacy and throughout the
pages are compelling stories of faith, courage,
and tenacity. It is definitely a best seller in my

gallery. I aspire everyday to live and breathe the principles espoused in the book.

Everybody stands to be blessed by this book. It addresses accountability on three main fronts: personal accountability touches on being accountable to self and holding oneself to a higher standard; accountability to others challenges both parental and leadership skills in assisting our children and followers to rise above the inevitable obstacles of life; accountability to God acknowledges that God ultimately gives the enabling power to reach our utmost destiny.

I recommend every household to have at least a copy of this book. It will positively impact the lot of anyone who will be bold and open minded enough to implement the basic principles suggested.

The author will welcome your kind and candid comments for future editions.

Enjoy.

Sunday Alaba Fawole, DDS, MD, MPH
CEO, Royal Wellness Center Inc., a non-profit Preventive Medicine Initiative

INTRODUCTION

Master of My Destiny is a book written from the depth of inner conviction by the author. You can find in it traces of things that the author herself has experienced. Hear her in her own words: "this book is written to bring encouragement and hope and to assure everyone that lives in this great country [America] that regardless of your unique circumstances and difficulties, with hard work, delayed gratification and perseverance, the sky is your limit and you can make it."

The book is a sincere reflection of her own challenges and struggles in God's own country, America and she also gives references to the lives of people like Paul Park, Colin Powell and a few Nigerians like Dr. Falase and Mr. Fawole. She concludes by saying it is not where you start that matters but where you end.

I am not surprised that she refers to the home as the untapped power house and the foundation of everyone's development, telling us categorically the effect that parents have on their children. This is because I know for sure that she is a wonderful mother, a great wife and an outstanding homemaker.

In chapter 7, "I Control my Financial Destiny", she tells us that the choices we make every day determine what we become. How true.

This book is almost a personal experience of survival in America. But it is a very good book for anyone who wants to live life and make a success of it anywhere. The language is honest, easy to understand and easy to follow. The personal experiences are most encouraging. In some sections, she does sound tough like a principled school teacher but with a lot of love. And, in essence, that's what my lovely author is: nice, hardworking, committed, dedicated, disciplined, principled, truthful and loving.

I recommend this as a must read.

PASTOR ITUAH IGHODALO
Trinity House, Lagos
Managing Partner, SIAO Professional Services
(2011)

Chapter One

The Battle is Waged from Within

That is, within the individual person, the individual family, the community. The tale is told of a wise, all-knowing old man who never made mistakes. And there was a young man who wanted to test the old man and question his wisdom. One day, the young man got a bird from the bush and placed it in his hand. He then asked the old man whether or not the bird was alive or dead. In his mind he thought, if the old man said the bird was alive, he would squeeze the bird dead. If the old man said the bird was dead, he would release the bird and let it go. Either way the old man would be proved a liar. The old man's response shocked him, "whether the bird lives or dies, the decision is in your hands."

This book is premised upon the fact that we all actually have it within us to succeed in many areas of our lives. We have the ability to make choices that will shape our destiny forever. Success is not only available for a privileged few who were raised with golden spoons in their mouths. And, by the way, success is much more than financial prosperity. Given the right resources, environment and support, a lot of us will make it in life. In order to thrive and reach our highest potential, most of us need a nurturing family, a supportive community and most importantly, a willingness to take responsibility for ourselves.

I firmly believe that if a child is raised in a nurturing environment with appropriate discipline, coupled with good parental example devoid of hypocrisy, the child has a good foundation to build on. Unfortunately, there are many children who will and have grown up without this privilege, or have deviated from the path they were introduced to. To those I say, be encouraged. You can start building from wherever you are. No matter how low you think you are, you can begin working towards your success, and you will achieve it. You can begin creating your own destiny, right now. Enough knowledge and resources are available if we would only use them.

The story of Joseph in the bible is illuminating. The bible records that Joseph prospered in Potiphar's house, as a slave! He was a slave, yet he was placed above everything and everyone in his master's house except the master's wife. Given his circumstances, he had a lot of reasons to be angry and disillusioned. He was poor, separated from his family and religion, maltreated and sold into slavery by his siblings! As if all that was not enough, he was unjustly thrown into prison, for what he did not do. How then did he end up becoming the king's right hand man? How did he become the man you had to know before you saw the king? Obviously, he did not get to Egypt, already knowing the right people. He had no godfathers to introduce him to the king. His was not a case of dad calling on his behalf and setting up interviews. He did not have the right last name. How did he do it? By being faithful to the task at hand, even though menial; by hard work, diligence and a high level of integrity. In spite of the injustice that took him to prison, he was still faithful and hardworking there. The result was that he did not remain a mediocre forever. As a matter of fact, he moved all the way to the top and became the Prime Minister of Egypt. (Please read the full story in the book of Genesis, chapters 39 through 41).

We can do no less if we are to succeed. The timeless values of hard work, tenacity, perseverance, integrity and faith are still the fuels for success. It will not be easy. The road to real and lasting success never is. But you can make it in life, regardless of your background or opportunity. My suggestions in this book are radical, and you may be uncomfortable with them or even get angry with me. I will be the first to admit that I am quite opinionated on issues that I believe in. But these are tried and tested principles, and they truly work. So, I encourage you to dig in, do it, and enjoy the rich rewards. You are the Master of your own destiny. Begin to create it, right now!

Chapter Two

The Story Behind the Glory

We see successful people around us all the time and we may sometimes envy them and wonder why everything seems to be going well for them. Most successful people however had to go through a lot of hardship before they made it in life. Many were not born with opportunities waiting for them. This quote from William Shakespeare's *Twelfth Night* is on point: " . . . Some are born great, some achieve greatness and some have greatness thrust upon them" (Acts II, Scene V). You might not have inherited greatness. You might not have been placed in an environment that will nurture greatness and make it happen. But we all can achieve greatness through our own individual effort.

In this chapter, you will read about a few immigrants from all walks of life and various situations. Some are professionals who came to this country already college educated but had to start from scratch in order to find their feet. Some had to change their course, go back to school and relearn what actually works in the society in which they have found themselves. Some only had high school or trade school education but have gone on to make something of themselves, using the resources available to them.

As varied as these experiences may seem to be, a common thread runs through. These people were in a strange land, often with little or no family support; most often did not qualify for government financial support, went through serious challenges and faced many obstacles, but made it! The playing field was level in the United States and even the highly educated immigrants were not at any advantage as they struggled for the same low paying jobs as their counterparts who did not come in with much education.

This book is written to bring encouragement and hope, and to assure everyone that lives in this great country that, regardless of your unique circumstances and difficulties, with hard work, delayed gratification and perseverance, the sky is your limit and you can make it. In Nigeria, we would often refer to America as

"God's Own Country" and we were right. When immigrants come to this wonderful country, they see opportunities flying all over, ready to be grabbed, and they grab them. This country is truly blessed, and everyone can make it here.

You will read below, the struggles of these immigrants as they tried to find lives for themselves in the United States and the seemingly insurmountable obstacles they had to overcome. But you will also read about their triumphs, which only came through the ageless values of tenacity, perseverance, endurance and faith.

Mr. Paul Parks immigrated to the United States from Korea several years ago while he was in his twenties with $100 to his name. He was not proficient in the English language and had to take English as a Second Language (ESOL) at a community college. At the same time, he worked as a bus boy at a hotel and enrolled in a University. He worked from 6pm to 2am and had to be ready to go to school at 7am. Due to his limited understanding of English, he sometimes stayed up all night learning the names of various wines.

Paul lived with his mother and sister who had been in the United States earlier but they could not help him financially. Mom was a part time bookkeeper and his sister was a full time student on school loans. Paul continued to work and go to school and, after 5 years, graduated as a Computer Scientist, got a job with AT&T, and bought his mom a house. Today, more than 20 years later, Paul lives a very successful life with his attorney wife and two wonderful children. His is an example of what anyone can achieve through hard work and perseverance even in the face of serious challenges.

Mr. Daniel Fawole emigrated from Nigeria about 9 years ago at about age 40 and without a college education. He left Nigeria with mixed feelings as he was leaving his wife and three sons behind. However, he thought more about the opportunities that he and his family could ultimately find in the United States.

He faced an initial challenge of not being able to drive, a situation that limited where he could live and work. He engaged in low paying jobs that he could find and enrolled in Nursing Assistant School. He worked two jobs and borrowed money from family and friends so he could bring his wife and children here to join him. Upon his family's arrival, he enrolled in Nursing School while still working full time. He also had his wife's financial support. Today, he is a Psychiatric Nurse, owns a home and drives, of course.

He is proud of the fact that in spite of the initial hardship, he promptly paid back his debt of close to $10,000 within his first year of arrival while still working at low paying jobs. He said his watchwords were trust, integrity and God's instruction in Romans 13:8 which says, "Owe no man anything . . . . " He credits his success to God's faithfulness, hard work, perseverance and strong family support.

Dr. Ekundayo Falase came to the United States in 1988 as an Obstetrician/Gynecologist from Nigeria for a two-year Fellowship program at the University of Pennsylvania. Even though he had practiced for many years in Nigeria, he had to complete a residency program in order to practice in the United States. An OB/GYN, he nonetheless had to work as a taxi driver in order to generate income while he studied for his board exams. He did not allow the fact that he was a doctor to prevent him from such a job.

Sometimes things take an unexpected turn in our lives and changes have to be made. Some of us have allowed even our education to be a stumbling block to our progress. Some of us sit at home with degrees that are not useful to us but we are not ready for the sacrifice involved in changing careers.

Dr. Falase went on to complete his residency, became board certified in Internal Medicine, and currently has his own medical practice, specializing in Nephrology and Hypertension. He said he was able to endure all the hardship he faced by standing on the promises of God.

Dr. Falase's wife, Oladapo Falase is a Registered Nurse from Nigeria and had also practiced for many years before relocating to the United States. She worked the night shift as a Nursing Assistant while she studied for her Nursing Board exam and took care of their two children during the day. She says she never resented her situation and always asked if there was anything more she could do even when her shift was over.

She worked with such diligence, joy and zeal as a Nursing Assistant that her co-workers were shocked when she passed her board exams to learn that she had been an RN the whole time! She said she had been brought up to do whatever her hand finds to do very well, and she knows that wherever she finds herself, God has a purpose for her being there and no trying situation will last forever. She is currently the Chief Operations Officer at their Medical Practice.

Dr. Oluyemi Badero attended High School in a small town in Nigeria where there was neither electricity nor pipe-borne water. The students drank well water and the school was powered by generators. More often than not, the students studied at night with candles and kerosene lanterns when there was no diesel to fuel the generators. Their principal always told them, "Look at what you have, not what you don't have. You have your syllabus and your teachers"—never mind that the senior class only had two teachers, one for Math and the other for Biology. Students had to read up on the other subjects by themselves. In spite of these serious limitations, Dr. Badero got straight As in all the nine subjects he took for the West African qualifying High School Graduation examination, fairing much better than many students who graduated from privileged schools.

Dr. Badero went on to become a Medical Doctor and practiced for a few years in Nigeria before a friend who lived in the United States challenged him to leave his comfort zone and come to America if he thought he was so smart. By the time he finally arrived in the US, his challenger had fallen on hard times, lost her job and apartment and was herself dependent on others. With only $500, two shirts and two pairs of pants to his name, Dr. Badero debated whether to accept defeat and return to Nigeria or stay, and rough things out. He chose the latter.

As can be expected, things were very difficult for him. He worked long hours doing menial jobs, depended largely on the largess of friends, and at times, did not have a place to stay. Today, he is a board certified interventional cardiologist of very high repute in New York and has won numerous awards including congressional recognition.

He says, "show me what someone has done, give me half the resources and I will achieve twice as much." He also has the strong belief that repeated success is by no means accidental, but is a result of certain principles and values that, if applied, will bring success every time.

General Colin Powell, former US National Security Advisor and Chairman of the Joint Chiefs of Staff, is well known to all of us. He is the son of Jamaican immigrants and so his story fits in here. I attended a seminar in 2010 where General Powell was one of the speakers. He told us that he attended the City College of New York and got out with a GPA of 2.0. He said his GPA came up to 2.0 only after the school added his Straight As in ROTC (Reserve Officers' Training Corps). He said the City College of New York could not wait to get rid of him. Of course he is now considered one of the best sons of the City of New York. He told us, "it's not where you start in life, but where you end up and what you do to get there." His life story tells it all. He shared three of the principles he lives by:

- "I don't miss anything in life"
- "I don't look at rear or side view mirrors"
- "I look forward to the next"

What incredible wisdom! Anyone who will succeed has to be focused and not distracted by the obstacles that life is sure to present. If you miss an opportunity, don't sit there worrying about it and letting it incapacitate you. Look forward to what you can do next.

With General Powell's academic background, who would have thought that he would rise up to be who he is today? He certainly took some steps to get there and those steps are worth finding out. One of the tasks that anyone who desires to succeed has to take on is read stories of successful people and what they had to go through to get to the top. We will find that in many cases, the path to success was not easy but it was not insurmountable.

Many of these people achieved success in spite of the obstacles they faced because they worked hard, persevered, and were willing to delay their gratification. Many did not have family support here, no godfathers to give them a jumpstart, no governmental aid, yet they succeeded, underscoring the fact that whether or not we succeed in life depends more on our own internal decisions and choices than on the environmental factors around us. And this may very well be the story of many successful immigrants and indigents alike. They are all worthy of emulation.

Chapter Three

The Untapped Powerhouse

𝕴 am speaking about the Home and I am getting ready to place an enormous responsibility on parents. This is not a book on parenting; however, this chapter still ends up being the longest one in the book and for good reason. The home and family have a lot to do with a person's preparation for life and success. Your children's destiny in life may very well depend on how you raise them. At some point in their lives, children are completely dependent on their parents for nurturing, training, guidance and even survival! We determine what food they eat, where they live, who they are exposed to, what they wear, what values they hold dear . . . the list goes on.

I remember telling people years ago that if I had a ten year old who was reported to be rude to a teacher, obnoxious and having no respect for authority, you could safely hold me responsible for that behavior. It is quite difficult for serious negative behavior to jump on a child all of a sudden if the child had been trained and had always acted a different way. The same way that it is difficult for a child that grew up with idleness, drug and alcohol abuse around him to naturally act differently as an adult, is the same way that it is difficult for a child raised under wholesome circumstances to enjoy a life of drunkenness later. It takes a lot of effort to act differently from your upbringing. Of course people are able to make things better for themselves regardless of how inadequate their backgrounds were; that is the whole point of this book. However, we all know what an uphill battle it is and how hard it is to rewire ourselves. Let's think about the following for a moment:

Parents determine whether or not their children are going to be good readers and determine what they read. In the book, "Gifted Hands: The Ben Carson Story" by Ben Carson and Cecil Murphey, the account is told of how Ben's mom, who only had a third grade education, made her children go to the library, read books and write reports that she herself couldn't read!

Ben eventually became an avid reader, thereby becoming an expert on many topics including names of rocks and changed from a dull child whom his classmates laughed at, to a very bright child, topping his class and today being a world renowned pediatric neurosurgeon. You will read that Ben Carson was already getting involved in street fights and was getting off to a very bad start that could have landed him in jail. However his lot was turned around by his mom insisting on him reading.

I determine for instance whether or not my children will do well in Math or not. It should be common knowledge that you have to actually put your hands on the paper and work on Math problems daily to really understand Math and do well in the subject. Do you have time in your day to make sure your child sits down to do Math problems and are you available to determine what their challenges are and what is in your power to meet those challenges?

My son was in third grade when he came home with a grade of 69% in Science one day. His sister in Middle School was furious! She made him bring his Science textbook home and drilled him over the next few days. She would not take no for an answer and made him study hard while she made herself available to answer his questions. My son had a 100% on his next Science test. Same child; same subject; same teacher; but completely different results. Receiving attention and guidance and having someone actually monitor his study made the difference. How many smart children have dropped out of school because no one gave them the personal attention they needed? You may sometimes have children that require more effort and attention than others. You have to recognize that and act accordingly. Given the right environment, every child can succeed.

I determine how my children will speak and what language they will embrace. What language do they hear at home growing up? Do you laugh when they bring bad language home or do you sincerely correct them? I remember us teaching our children that phrases and words such as "shut up" and "stupid" were undesirable and were not accepted in our home. Of course we made sure that we did not use them either. I remember that whenever we went out and the children heard someone say "stupid" they cringed, covered their faces and whispered, "Oh! She said the bad word!" Their reaction was quite hilarious to watch but it underscored the fact that children only know what they are exposed to. How careful we must be then in choosing what we expose them to.

I determine whether or not my children will play Sports. If you want them to play sports, you will enroll them in a team, buy uniforms for them and actually take them to practice.

I determine whether or not they will play the piano, another instrument or none at all. If I really want them to play the piano, I will have a keyboard for them to practice on, get a piano teacher for them and pay for their lessons. I will also make sure they practice every day. Keep up with the routine and you are sure to have children who will grow up playing the piano. You made it happen because of what you did.

I determine whether or not they'll know how to be respectful because I will teach them, show them, and expect compliance.

You get the point. A large percentage of what children will become is determined in the home. The government and the society cannot do or undo much about it. Many of the activities our children engage in (or do not engage in), at least when they are young and at home, are determined by parents. What choices do we make for them? What values of life do we present and portray to them? What exposures do we give them?

We had a function the other day that my two older daughters travelled from their school to attend. As soon as both of them arrived, they sprang into action and made themselves useful, filling in gaps and helping out where necessary. We kept sending them back and forth and they ran errands willingly and without complaining. I sent them a text the following day telling them that I was so proud of them and that they were the best children ever. They each responded that they thanked me for raising children that I could be proud of. They passed the compliment right back to me. As we lay our bed in raising our children, so shall we lie on it.

From time to time people talk about parents who raised their children right but the children went their own ways. Situations like these do in fact exist because ultimately, the children still have to make their own choices, but I will like to think that they are the exception rather than the rule. Sometimes also, we might think we are using the right approach in raising our children and we may not be. I am a firm and obstinate believer in the fact that God is faithful and will not fail in His promise that if we train our children in the way that they should go, they will not depart from it (Proverbs 22:6). If we have done our part and the result is still not pleasing, we turn them back to God on our knees and He will turn them around so that His promise will still come to pass as He does not lie.

Some people may judge me idealistic and say that my suggestions only work with middle class folks. My response is two-fold. First, if all the people we consider middle class will practice what has been proposed, there will still be a huge impact because the problems of lack of motivation in our society is not limited to the poor or low socioeconomic class. If we have more people doing the right thing, then we will have more people impacting others. Secondly, this is not a move to change America or the world in one day. As many of us as possible just need to take the first step. Then and only then can we hope for change down the road. After all, it is a common saying that the definition of insanity is doing the same thing the same way and expecting a different result.

Parenting is such an important job that it behooves us to be as prepared as we can before embarking on this very important journey. It is amazing how everyone knows you cannot practice any profession without prior education and/or experience but when it comes to parenting, most of us think we can just jump into it, without any preparation. Please lay your hands on any resource that offers help in this area, and keep on learning, all through the years of raising your children. I will discuss below some strategies we adopted that I believe really helped us in raising our children.

The Need to Have a Backbone

In the world of parenting, we have to be firm. You may have heard the popular saying, "Parenting is not for Wimps." That is such a true saying in my opinion. When you promise your child a punishment after certain misbehavior, you better follow through with it. Better to promise a punishment you can live with, than to promise and not deliver. Sometimes you suffer a lot of anguish as you punish your children because you love them so much and really do not want them to be sad in any way. However, you have to do it now, so you and they can enjoy a life of peace and happiness later. In the midst of everything you do, let your love for your children be constant, unconditional and very apparent to them.

I am blessed to have a firm but loving mother. She did not wince at all when she had to punish you. But afterwards, she would pull you to herself and explain to you again why she had to do what she did. I remember growing up, I might have done something that warranted getting spanked. Some Good Samaritan might have been visiting, who tried to convince my mom not to spank me. Mom would say, "I had wanted to give her six strokes before, but because of your intervention, I'll reduce it to four. However, she is not going to get off without anything." Of course there are many different ways of disciplining your children and spanking is only one of them, but you have to know when and how to do it. There definitely is a right and wrong way. But if the bible says "spare the rod and spoil the child?"(Proverbs 13:24), then I know the "if" question is settled, I just have to know how to do it right.

Children do not enjoy being disciplined. My now, highly responsible, caring and sweet 23 year old daughter once told me when she was about 15 years old that my husband and I were too controlling and were not happy when our children didn't do exactly as we asked. Well, hello??? Of course we didn't like it when they disobeyed. What parent does? She was also the one that cried and wailed as if her world was coming to an end when we did not allow her to do a sleep over with one of her friends when she was 14 years old. She reflected on the incident one day when she was about 18 years old and said she couldn't believe she cried over that situation. She said, "that was so stupid. It's not that serious!" Sometimes we have to act the adult that we are and make certain unpopular decisions for our children. Their understanding will catch up with ours later.

Parenting Support Group

Parenting support group is a wonderful idea, and you can never invest too much in your children. You get ideas from other parents regarding your struggles and you exchange ideas.

Teachable Moments

You must take advantage of Teachable Moments. They are powerful. This may happen when there is some tragic news on TV about what happened to a child or young person. I remember a story many years ago about a teenager whose parents thought was in bed at 3am but had actually sneaked out to attend a party. When the police came to break the news of the child's death through a car crash to her parents, they insisted there was a mistake as their teenager was sleeping upstairs. Of course they were wrong! I know this story haunted our first daughter for a long time, and even now, she still says, "I know I would be the one to get into trouble if I sneaked to do something like that." Of course you don't have to wait for such a tragic situation to teach your children.

Family Meetings

Family meetings are great tools for happy and cohesive families. We try to have it once a month, and definitely before the children return to school after the holidays. As the children got older, they actually moderated and drew up the agenda. It is an opportunity where we commend each child for whatever achievements or positive things we have observed, and also to point out where improvements are needed. We share the plans and concerns we have for the family; share issues facing the family for which we all need to pray and so on. The list goes on but you get the idea. You make one that suits your family. Most importantly, the children get to tell us what issues they have with us and they know that in this forum, they are free to say whatever is on their minds. Of course respectful delivery is always expected.

Expect Respect from your Child

Children are not parents and it is unfortunate when we allow them to rule over us. Driving for instance is a privilege for them. Most of the time, we are the ones that either teach them how to drive or pay for a lesson; we own the car they start off with, and they still slap us in the face with this privilege. I remember when one of our daughters was going to go for her Driving test. It was the summer following her High School graduation and she so much wanted to obtain her license before starting college. Well, the evening before her scheduled date for the test, I was at work talking to her on the phone and determined that she was rude to me during our conversation. I told her there and then, that she could forget about me taking her for any test the following day. She knew I was not joking. She was awake when I got home late that night, begging me and crying. I told her not to waste her tears because I was not changing my mind. Of course when I told my husband, he agreed with me and stated that our daughter got what she deserved. She ended up taking the test a few months later after she was well in college. The lesson was well learned.

Parents must cooperate in Discipline

That brings me to the point of how much cooperation is needed between parents in the raising of our children. A whole book could be written on this. Children are very smart and could be manipulative. If they sense disagreement between the parents, they'll often look for, and find a place to hide. Our children used to cause disagreements between my husband and I until I understood their tricks. They would ask dad for something, and, if he said, "No," they would come to me, and I might say, "Yes," not knowing they had talked to my husband. So then I learned to ask them, "Have you asked daddy?" "What did he say?" "So why are you coming to me?" Sometimes you might disagree with the way one of you is handling a particular situation. You should discuss the issue with your spouse, but never in the presence of your children. They should always know you agree in their discipline. Of course we have the abnormal situation where there is an abusive parent. In that situation, the other parent cannot be quiet and look on, and professional help should be sought.

I know the situation gets a bit more complex when parents are separated and the children have to be in two different homes where there may be two different ways of doing things. In instances like this, I hope parents would agree that even though they may not like each other anymore, they both love their children and want the best for them. They should therefore put their differences aside, approach this in a mature manner, and agree not to undermine each other's efforts in training their children. Sometimes the non-custodial parent might want to overcompensate and spoil the children during the few moments he or she has with them. This would not be right or beneficial to the child.

Once we communicate with our children and let them know where we are coming from, and we combine our discipline with love, children are smart and will understand. I know I have oversimplified a very complex situation. A lot of assistance is needed here and you should seek all the help you need. You will be amazed at what resources are out there in books, internet and so on. Let us avail ourselves.

All throughout this book you will come across radical suggestions. I can only share what I have; what I have tried and tested; what has worked for us; what I trust.

Family Devotions

By far the most powerful concept that has helped us in parenting our children is the idea of Family Devotions. It is our family time, and, by the way, every family needs a time of coming together every day. It's one of those little, seemingly insignificant things that go a long way in forging home harmony. I know we are all busy outside doing other things and helping other people, but nothing will help us better in achieving the success that we all desire in our families.

To the glory of God, we have meaningful family devotions every morning and evening. Our children in High School get on the school bus at 6:30am; hence, we are all sitting at devotion by 6:10am. Everyone knows to be in the living room at that time, no sleeping-in. And, if we parents are out of town, or do not come downstairs for prayer on time, the children begin and have devotion on their own. We spend about 15 minutes singing a hymn, reading scripture, and reading from our chosen devotional for the year. We close with our Family Creed/Confession (more on this later). The children take turns leading out in devotions. My husband and I may add our two cents at the end of it. We are always discussing with the children and reviewing our devotional styles all the time. The last thing you want is for your family devotions to become monotonous, mere routine or a meaningless tradition.

We carefully and prayerfully choose the devotionals we use and make sure they are relevant to the situations and issues facing their age group. A particularly good one we came across a few years ago was "Sticky Situations" by Betsy Schmitt. The devotional addresses almost every situation that a school age kid will experience, all the way through High School, and explores the various choices available for facing the challenges. I think the children appreciate the fact that the issues they face are universal, and that there are always constructive ways of dealing with them.

One beautiful tradition we have with our morning devotion is our family creed or confession. We read it right before we have the closing prayer. We selected promises from the Bible that address protection, self-esteem, and the children's responsibility as children of God. We were especially led to do it after the schools became very unsafe for kids with students coming in with guns and so on. Before we actually started using it, we had a family meeting where we went through each verse in various bible translations so that the children had an understanding of what they were reading. We then typed it out in the King James Version and every one had a copy. After a few weeks, we discovered that no one needed the paper anymore. We all had it memorized without making any conscious effort to do so. We leave the scripture references out when we read our creed and I think that made it easier. We have since given copies to many of our family and friends. I think it is great for every family to come up with their own verses and what they think is relevant and meaningful to them. However, I will share ours below:

FAMILY CREED / CONFESSION

*This is the day that the lord hath made,
I will rejoice and be glad in it.
Psalm 118:24*

*Behold, I am for signs and for wonders in this
land, and wherever I go.
Isaiah 8:18*

*I am being trained in the way I should go,
when I am old, I will not depart from it in
Jesus' name. Proverbs 22:6*

*I am taught of the Lord, and great shall be my
peace. Isaiah 54: 13*

*Surely, goodness and mercy shall follow me
today, and all the days of my life, and I shall
dwell in the house of the Lord forever. Psalm
23:6*

*No weapon that is formed against me shall
prosper, and every tongue that shall rise
against me in judgment,
I shall condemn in the name of Jesus. Isaiah
54:17*

*I shall not die but live, and declare the works
of the Lord. Psalm 118:17*

*The Lord will satisfy me with long life, and
show me his salvation.
Psalm 91:16*

*I will serve the Lord my God, and he shall
bless my food and water, and the Lord will
take all sickness from me, the number of my
days I will fulfill. Exodus 23:25, 26*

*But we are a chosen generation, a royal
priesthood, a holy nation, a peculiar people,
that we may show forth the praises of Him,
who hath called us out of darkness into his
marvelous light. 1 Peter 2:9*

The children are thus sent off to school with
the word of God, prayer, positive affirmations,
and fresh, verbal reminders of the children of
whom they are.

You can never be too busy to find time to
have devotion with your children. I remember a
very busy and stressful time in our lives when
my husband sometimes left home as early
as 5am and I may have worked through the
night, not getting home till around 8am. The
children got together in our absence anyway,

and had devotion before going to school because the tradition was already in place. Needless to say, being able to get up early enough to have meaningful family devotions means strict enforcement of bedtime.

We have more time during our evening devotion—30 to 45 minutes depending on how good it gets. We use another devotional and get to discuss various issues. It's our family time and we love it! Most of all however, we encourage our children to have their own personal devotions. It is extremely important that they know God for themselves. We encourage them to find a suitable time in their busy schedules to accommodate this and we find appropriate resources to help them in this regard.

Let me pause here to say that they are not always going to enjoy or appreciate getting up so early for devotions. But, you always have to keep your goal and end-result in sight. When you do what you have to do, the dividends are priceless and you get to enjoy your peace early and for a long time. If you are having trouble with your child's behavior, it may be time to add family devotions to your daily routine. The Lord who created us knows just what is best for us.

God is faithful and you can never go wrong following His instructions. Family devotion time is His brilliant idea. In Deuteronomy chapter

6, verses 6-9, the bible says we should teach our children God's word at every opportunity, not just during daily devotions. It means using every teachable moment to instruct our children throughout the day as mentioned earlier. Sometimes some news on TV will be the topic of our devotion that evening. Sometimes we stop a family movie mid-stream to get some things straight! I remember one time we were watching "Free Willy" when the children were much younger. We got to a scene where Willy was rude to his mom and slammed the door while she was talking to him. We stopped the movie and had a whole discussion about that and I reminded the children of how that was still a No-No in our home, in case they had forgotten. They said, "yes, we know that! We know that! But can we get back to the movie please?" I responded, "Yes, of course we will. I just want to be sure we are all clear on this."

Never too late to Change

As you contemplate on all the above, you may feel that you should have started this when the children were little and that it is probably too late now. No! No! All through the years, we have gained knowledge about better ways of doing things—healthier ways of eating, etc. We'll call the children together, let them know about the new gem we have found, and we let them know we are obligated as their parents to walk in the new path that we know will benefit them. Thorough explanation to the children is extremely important. You can't just lord it over them. You also have to be very patient with one another as you seek to change routines. But, yes, it can and must be done, if necessary. We cannot be slaves to old, ineffective and injurious ways of doing things because we are afraid to introduce change to our families.

Children may take you on a guilt trip too. "But, mom, we've always done it this way; why are you making us change now?" And my response is, "I know better now, and I cannot be a slave to my tradition."

Foster Unity among the Children

We need to do all we can to foster unity and cohesiveness among our children as they will serve as support system for one another later on. Having siblings as support systems could save many young people from giving up on life when hard times come.

Parents have a lot to do with whether or not their children will be friends of one another. Every child is different, and it may sometimes be easier to love one child more than the other but playing favoritism is the surest way to sow discord among siblings. The real test of parenting comes when we are able to go the extra mile in helping the academically challenged or less obedient child rather than taking the line of least resistance and gravitating towards the child that pleases us.

Teach Self Control

We also need to guard against raising selfish children, especially in this affluent land of ours. I once had a coworker who said she grew up so poor that she determined she was going to give her children anything they wanted. She lamented, "I ended up raising selfish children." I made up my mind there and then about some things that would not happen with our children. My husband and I are opposed to our children each having a television set in their rooms and so they do not. When they were really young, we only had television in the living room. They all had to crowd around the couch and watch together. If one wanted to watch a show, and another child wanted the other, they had to find a way of compromising so that each child's needs would be met at one time or another. We were not going to give each child a TV just because three children wanted to watch three different programs at the same time. We told them it would make absolutely no difference if we ever became millionaires. Our decision was based on principle, not affordability. We only had a computer in the living room for everyone's use also. There are things that we should not give our children, even if we could afford them.

The rules of course changed when our children started college and had laptops. They had the opportunity of doing their own thing if they didn't want to be with the rest of the family. The seed had been sown at the right time though, hence, even now, they will rather still be together. In spite of the age difference between them, our four children are very close to one another, thoroughly enjoy one another's company, and watch out for one another. We have to be careful not to allow affluence to take away survival tools from our children.

Live What You Preach

It is extremely important for us not to be hypocrites. We must practice what we preach otherwise we will lose our children. No matter what we say, they will always be influenced more by what we do. It is hard to do but let us do our best and the Lord will bless our meager efforts. Can you imagine how a child feels when he observes a parent who is a bully and a disagreeable person at home suddenly turn to an angel in church? I don't know what could be more damaging to a child or what more could prepare them for rebellion.

Talking about church, some people wonder how their children went astray even though they were taken to church every week. Was the child really in church though? Be sure your child is in church and listening too. Too often I see children sitting away from their parents, talking to their friends and missing everything they need to hear. Some would be outside the building talking to their friends during the sermon. We required that our children sit with us throughout their young years. When they would plead with us to allow them sit with their friends, we would ask them to invite their friends and we would all sit together. We required this until they started college. It was interesting though that even after they were in college and came home on holidays, they voluntarily sat with us.

The Family that Plays Together . . .

Have family fun time together. Find activities that you all enjoy and do them. We love sitting around just bonding and joking around, watching family movies, playing board games together and most of all traveling. The night before a trip, hardly any of the children goes to sleep from excitement.

At the last marriage retreat we attended, the presenters shared the idea of weekly family fun. We came home and implemented it immediately but we adopted a biweekly schedule (every other Monday evening at 7pm) so as not to disturb the children's studies. One member of the family chooses an activity that the whole family will do. The next time, it's another member's turn to choose. It's only fun activity. Nothing study related, except that when it was my husband's turn the first time, he chose Scrabble (*Go Figure!*). The family fun night idea has resonated very well with our children and I am sure every child would love it.

Be a Praying Parent

Finally, it's not being a perfect parent, because no one can ever be; it's being a praying parent. I could not say it better than Stormie Omartian in her book, "The Power of a Praying Parent." I recommend it as a 'must read' for every parent. We need the Lord to bless our efforts. "Except the Lord builds the house, they labor in vain that build it." Psalms 127:1.

Chapter Four

No One Can Hinder You But You

𝕴 am getting ready to delve into a very touchy subject; that of race relations in America and how it has been a source of hindrance to many. It is an issue that is frequently and inappropriately utilized by both sides of the spectrum. There is a tendency on the part of some black people to blame white people for their problems while some white people tend to stereotype black people and make incorrect assumptions.

I will not deny the fact that racism exists because we still have a lot of ignorant people around. And it is a subject that is not lacking in focus or cognizance in any way as everybody uses it. I once worked in an office where the majority of the employees were black. We had a black female employee that was not friendly and hardly interacted with anyone. At some point she had to pair up on a project with one of the few white employees. The white employee came to a few of us one day, completely frustrated with her partner. She said very seriously, "I guess she doesn't like me because I am white." It was laughable. I had to ask her if she had never noticed this lady in the office before her own encounter. It is just so easy for us to make racism the culprit for all our woes so that the real issues are ignored and unaddressed.

If all I am going to do is reiterate the reality of racism however, I will be bringing nothing new to the table and, stating the obvious without doing more is of no benefit to anyone. This book is about doing what you can, with what you have. Even in the midst of all the ills in our society, we all can take steps to succeed and hold our heads high.

It is very disheartening to see various negative statistics about blacks; consistently underperforming educationally, more disproportionately represented in the prisons and so on. My belief is that as a people, we need to move to the next step in dealing with these issues.

Thank God for the battles fought and still being fought in the courts, the legislatures, in the schools, on the streets, churches, media and so on. History bears witness to the great exploits and sacrifices of men and women to right wrongs and increase opportunities for everyone. Praise God for all that was done and continues to be done to bring freedom to all. These efforts are laudable and need to continue. However, in order for these efforts to yield lasting results, a lot has to be done at the individual level. The final push needed to tip us over; the step that will cross the finish line and bring victory has to come from within.

Following a leader who will be the spokesperson is wonderful but will not be sufficient today. And, as a matter of fact, leaders who always point accusing fingers at others will not help us. We need to be made aware of what is in our power to make things better for us. We must beware of leaders who retell or refer to history in a way that invokes self-pity, and/or rage, emotions that are not only negative but incapacitating. Leaders should propel us to take what we have from this point and move forward.

What have we done with all the rights and privileges that are ours so far? How have we maximized them? History of course is important and must not be ignored. That is why Winston Churchill said in his wisdom: "If we open up a quarrel between the past and the present, we shall find we have lost the future." History is excellent for learning and for making the future better, but not for retaliation or continued dependence.

Some of us continue to blame our failures on the color of our skin, social and economic standing, lack of education, and so on and so on. While the effect of all the above cannot be nullified or underestimated, the relevant fact for us is that we can overcome the obstacles plaguing our way and indeed we must.

There is an African adage that, translated means "He who seeks to destroy one only teaches one how to be strong." Talk about self-motivation! Even if we are convinced that there is a system that seeks to pull us down, that in itself should be the impetus that actually propels us towards success.

While not in any way denying or undermining the reality of discrimination and racism, I will nevertheless like to offer a different perspective on the issue. Coming from the vantage point of growing up in Nigeria, where the tribal discriminations are just as bad if not worse than the racial tensions here, it is easier for me to take a more objective view. Having also had the privilege of attending a multiracial church here in the United States for a few years, I have been able to discover that human beings are essentially the same. When it comes down to the basic needs of life, we all have the same issues, concerns, fears and so on. We are really not as different as we think we are.

Also, when we think about the frustrations and injustices that we might be experiencing, we need to take time to remember that white people were very much involved and were very often important catalysts in the breakthroughs that were accomplished. Many sacrificed their lives and that of their families alongside with black people during the civil rights era. Many white judges made honest and fair rulings that corrected wrongs. The Supreme Court decision that desegregated schools was by a panel of nine white male justices.

Everyone is probably familiar with the story of Michael Oher, a homeless black boy who became a professional football player with the Baltimore Ravens, thanks in large part to the wonderful white family who took him in. Michael was a poor homeless boy, wearing a t-shirt and cutoff jeans and walking in the snow when he was spotted by a white lady named Leigh Anne Tuohy. She and her husband, Sean took Michael in to their home, and, together with their children, loved him into a whole new life of wellbeing and great success. You can read about this incredible story in the book, "The Blind Side" by Michael Lewis.

I do not cease to be amazed at the way Americans respond to request for aid all across the world including predominantly black countries. If you watched the news during the last catastrophic earthquake event in Haiti, you would notice that there were workers from all over the world including Americans in their various skin colors and there were notably more white people in the rescue teams. I remember the story of a white lady from Florida who lost a leg during the effort. We cannot ignore or deny these facts.

How about missionaries who left their comfort zone and took the good news to Africa? I know that some people have also talked about some negative aspects of that whole situation. However, being an African immigrant myself, I can appreciate that it takes a lot of agape love to leave the United States and live in Africa especially knowing what Africa would have been like a century or more ago. We recently celebrated the 90th birthday of Dr. Sherman Nagel who was a missionary to Nigeria many decades ago. You could not convince the hundreds of Nigerians who celebrated in Texas that evening that this white man was not going to have uncountable number of stars in his crown when he got to heaven for the mighty works of mercy and love that he did in Nigeria.

I have also worked with a number of white judges and it has frankly amazed me to see how extremely fair and impartial they are, contrary to common societal belief. And how about my first-hand knowledge of "all white" jury panels declaring black defendants "not guilty" more times than you might believe since that is not what the media portrays. Or, white attorneys zealously and genuinely defending their indigent, court assigned black clients.

Look around and think about your own experience. If you think deeply, I have no doubt that you have experienced many gracious encounters with people of different races. Many of the teachers who have shown genuine interest and have positively impacted our black children's lives have been white. My white next door neighbor's yard is a place where all the kids in the neighborhood in their various hues come to play basketball. He comes home and shoots the hoops right along with them. And the kids have been given the freedom to play there even when the residents are out of town on vacation.

The moral of the story is; black or white, no one must be judged by the color of his or her skin; a powerful call declared in the unforgettable speech of the great MLK Jr.

All the negative statistics about African Americans certainly give the impression of having been given a bad deal. The only problem is; continuing to use racism as an excuse prevents us from looking internally for other causes and therefore, appropriate solutions. I will never forget an experience I had when my first daughter was in fourth grade about fourteen years ago. I had been hearing complaints from other parents about how the teacher had a hard time teaching because of so many unruly children disrupting the class. I decided to visit the class one day to observe. I watched as a young boy in the class threw tantrums and refused to follow the teacher's instructions. I pulled him aside and asked him what the matter was. He told me the teacher did not like him because he was black and she was white. He was only nine years old! I had further discussion with him and tried to show him what other factors might be causing the problems between him and his teacher other than racism. Unfortunately, he was probably repeating what he had heard so many times at home.

I taught High School Biology for a few years and often use that experience as an object lesson for my children. There is no teacher who would not take a liking to a child who follows instruction, and is courteous, respectful and hardworking. That child would receive the teacher's assistance even if he or she has a hard time understanding the concepts taught. On the other hand, a rude and obnoxious child, even if brilliant, would not receive the teacher's award.

You are well aware of tribal wars in Africa that have frequently led to genocide and other horrible crimes. The participants are all black but still find ways that they are different enough not to be able to live together in peace. There is police brutality in Nigeria where the perpetrator and the victim have the same skin color and belong to the same tribe. The rich man's son gets the job while the poor man's more qualified son does not. How about the caste and class system in India and the horrible repercussions? I could go on and on about different forms of discrimination in other societies that have the same if not more damaging effects than racism and discrimination in America. Wherever you live on earth, humans will find a way to discriminate among themselves. But we cannot allow the behavior of others to determine what we will do with our lives.

What we have tried to impart to our children is to approach every person and situation with an open mind and be ready to take responsibility. They know they could never give the excuse of "my teacher doesn't like me" or, "my teacher doesn't teach well" as a reason for failing a test. Whatever happened to getting the textbook and reading it for yourself? Make no mistake about it. You will still experience discrimination and injustice because we live in an imperfect world, but you choose how you allow that to affect you—either to propel you forward or drag you down. You choose.

I am also sure that many of us have experienced worse treatment from people who share our skin color. I once worked in an office with a black boss and mostly black employees where the experience was less than optimal. I later transferred to another office where my boss was white and so were most of the employees. It was a wonderful work environment and the black employees felt very comfortable.

We need to deal with everyone with an open mind and give people a benefit of the doubt. It is time to take the winning step in dealing with how we have been treated in the past and how to make our lives and that of our progeny better in the future.

It is a fact of course that black people are disproportionately represented in the criminal justice system and in the prisons. And there are factors responsible for that, some of which involve economics and education, or the lack of it, situations which also plague the black community disproportionately. Thankfully, these are situations that we have the power to change, from within us as individuals, families and communities, so that this does not continue to be our lot.

We have frequently seen in our society that when children grow up in poor neighborhoods and live in poverty, their performance in school is directly proportional. That is, they have the poor test scores and often the parents are not proactive in their children's learning. Growing up in Nigeria, however, where everyone basically believed that the road to success in life was education, it did not matter how poor and uneducated the parents were; they still believed in education and would do without, and make whatever sacrifices needed in order to secure the best education for their children.

Sometimes we also make the mistake of thinking that children are dumb just because they are poor. Nothing could be farther from the truth. There are so many intelligent kids in poor neighborhoods and schools who would thrive and soar if they would receive the attention they need. The efforts of big brother big sister and, going into our communities to educate both parents and children while providing mentoring are commendable and should continue. We are taking mastery of our own destiny when we engage in such efforts.

As black people, we can be our own worst enemies. When blacks kill blacks, who is responsible for that? When a teenage girl runs around with boys instead of staying in school and gets pregnant, whose fault is that? When men make babies and abscond their responsibility, who is to blame for that? I encourage men to rise up to the occasion and be whom God has called you to be—the head of your homes. Being an absent, uninvolved father is not a black thing. Being a selfless provider and a priest in your home earns you the respect you need and deserve.

I thank God for a father who was faithful in following God's blueprint in the conduct of his home. He is a loving husband and a dutiful father. A highly respected spiritual leader, we never missed morning and evening devotion in my home growing up. Dad is a veteran High School Principal and served as the President of All Nigeria Conference of Principals of Secondary Schools for two 4-year terms. He went on to hold an executive position with the Teaching Service Commission and finally retired as the Chief Executive Director of a non-profit foundation that serviced the whole nation. These were apart from his services as a community leader and his duties as Church Elder. His tight schedule never got in the way of his commitment to his family. What was most important though, and what actually kept my siblings and I in the path was his consistency. He was not a hypocrite. The faithful man you saw on the street corner was the same man in the closet. He was God's representative in our eyes and we hated to disappoint this man who lived what he preached. His attitude was enough to convict us. A child's destiny is very much tied to the influence of the father in the home.

I pray that our black men will rise up to their duties and I look forward to the day when being a black boy in the United States will be synonymous with being smart and confident. It is a dream but it has a great potential for coming true if we drastically change our paradigm and indeed we must. I am optimistic that if we know what we need to do, and actually do it, we will dramatically improve and eventually reverse the plight of black people in America.

Let me of course be balanced and state that there are a lot of black men doing the right thing. I have been to a lot of black churches and communities and personally know a lot of black men who are responsible fathers and are very prominent heads of their homes and communities. It was at a seminar where a 79 year old articulate black man told us that he got his PhD at age 75 that I made up my mind to work harder at completing this book even if I don't get a PhD. I believe that responsible black men are the majority but the bad eggs always steal the show and get talked about more.

In his book, "Black Rednecks and White Liberals" Thomas Sowell points out that a lot of what is referred to as black culture today did not originate with blacks but was simply a southern culture and way of life. He states that the key to upward economic mobility is education, and that hard work, thriftiness and education mark the attitude of successful people anywhere regardless of race.

I invite you to examine the poem below written decades ago by one of Nigeria's foremost educators, Pa J. F. Odunjo, and see how very right Thomas Sowell is on that issue. The poem was written in the Yoruba language and is entitled, **"Ise ni ogun ise."** It was translated into English by Professor Quansy Salako in order to teach Yoruba children in the diaspora. It is a poem that all elementary school children in the Western Region of Nigeria had to learn when I was growing up. I hope the English language does justice to this masterpiece that served to shape the thinking and lives of millions of children in that part of the world. The poem extols education and hard work and, translated into English is entitled:

"WORK IS THE ANTIDOTE FOR POVERTY"

Work Hard my friend
Hard work takes you to a position of honor and respect
If we do not have anyone to lean on, we appear indolent
If we do not have anyone to depend on, we simply work harder
Your mother may be wealthy
Your father may have a ranch full of horses
If you depend on their riches
You will end up in disgrace, I tell you
Whatever gain one does not work hard to earn
Usually does not last
Whatever one works hard for
Is what lasts in one's hands
Your arm is your relative while your elbow is your sibling
You may be loved by the world today
But it is only if you have money
That they will love you tomorrow
Or when you are in a high position
All will honor you with cheers and smiles

Wait till you become poor and struggling to get
by
And see how all grimace at you as you pass by
Education also puts one in a position of
leadership
Work hard to acquire a good one
And if you see a lot of people mocking
education
Please do not emulate them or keep their
company
Suffering is lying in wait for an unserious kid
Sorrow is in reserve for a truant kid
Do not play with your early years, my friend
Work hard, time and tide wait for no one

It is personally very disturbing and disconcerting to me to see statistics about black children consistently performing lower than other ethnic groups in America. Some people have actually ventured to say that blacks are genetically inferior. I beg to seriously differ. I grew up in Africa and went to school with very smart people, some of whom have proceeded to the United States and have consistently performed excellently in their various vocations.

I remember a young lady, Dr. Ife Adepoju, who came from Nigeria a few years ago as a teenager, wanting to continue her education at the 10th grade level here. She was told that she belonged in 9th grade because of her age. The school however had to agree with her when she took the 10th grade test and scored 100% in all subjects. She is in her 4th year of Surgery Residency today and plans to be a plastic surgeon. I also know about many African American children excelling in various academic areas in High Schools, Colleges and Universities. Many of them are in the Ivy League schools all across this country.

When you also think about the fact that, in black countries of the world, all their teachers, police officers, doctors, top company executives, presidents, and every other "good thing" is black, then you know that obviously, inferior genetic disposition of the black race is not an issue. What makes the difference is in the environmental influences, exposure and expectations that each family places on its own. Things we can control. Things we can change. And that has nothing to do with race.

When we had our children, there was no question about whether or not they would go to college. What other option is there? It mattered not what the statistics were or what the society predicted for them. They were college bound! To the glory of God, our first two daughters, Fiyin and Ope, are in medical school; our son, Gbolu is a freshman Engineering major in college, and our last daughter, Damisi is a junior in High School. They have all attended and still attend Public Schools, a privilege guaranteed to every child in America. They are not geniuses by any stretch of the imagination, just children who received love and attention and were not allowed to slack off. We did not leave the work for their teachers alone but made it our business to know what was going on with them and their studies. In their situation, they are fortunate that even their grandparents are college graduates. But even if that were not the case, we would not expect less from them, knowing fully well that education will jumpstart anyone in any society.

I attended a High School Graduation ceremony where the guest speaker asked the graduates to repeat the only two options they had. The options were, "either I'm going to make it or, I'm going to make it." Those were the only two options. I loved it!

Even when parents are not educated, they can aim high for their children and make whatever sacrifices they need to make in order to better their children's lives. I mentioned Mrs. Carson earlier. She had a third grade education and was poor. Yet she made up her mind that her children were going to grow up to live in the same kinds of large homes that she cleaned. And her wish came to pass, probably in larger magnitude than she had imagined. One of her sons, Ben Carson, a pediatric neurosurgeon as I mentioned earlier, travels across the globe to perform spectacular, one-of-a-kind surgeries. He made medical history in 1987 when he became the first surgeon in the world to successfully separate Siamese twins conjoined at the back of the head! Did I mention that Dr. Ben Carson is black? If there is any country where you can make your dreams come true, it's the United States of America. So, what's stopping you? What are you waiting for?

Let us put our efforts in the right direction. It is better to spend money on a tutor than buying designer and name brand outfits for our children. Better to live more simply so we can work less hours and spend the time paying attention to our children's grades and how to keep them up. Let us give our children the gift that will really make a difference and one that truly matters.

This book is not an academic treatise or a political paper. It does not seek to argue issues or put forth the results of any research. But I share practical solutions that work regardless of what society they are practiced in. They are the ingredients for success anywhere. They are things that every individual has the power to put in place; principles that many have used and obtained successful results. If as many families as possible will follow these principles and train more to do the same, we will raise a next generation that will begin to change the stereotype of what it means to be a black child in this society. How I look forward to the day!

Chapter Five

Lessons from Mom's Lips

𝕸y mom had many wise sayings that she frequently pronounced while we were growing up. They were so powerful that they shaped our lives in so many ways and we never forgot them. Of course they are common sayings but she used them very often and very liberally.

She is an action lady and a go-getter. A Registered Nurse and a Midwife, she nonetheless owned a hospital for over 40 years and employed doctors including a surgeon expatriate from India. Nigeria's economy was great back then. When Dr. Varghese arrived, he had a newly built 3-bedroom house and a brand new car waiting for him and when he left after four years, he shipped a lot of goodies back to India. Here are some of mom's favorite quotes:

"Buy what you need and not what you want" . . . when school was about to resume and you brought your long list of 'needs'

"Five minutes enjoyment, everlasting sorrow" . . . when she gave instructions and counseled us on the need for sexual purity

"Decency is no pride" . . . Mom is very fashionable and a firm believer that dressing well and looking nice do not suggest that one is proud

"Delay is Dangerous" . . . She is an action lady and this was her counsel against procrastination. She would say, "what you can do today, don't leave till tomorrow"

"Be like a pair of scissors; whatever comes between you, cut it" . . . her favorite advice to newlyweds

"I have no matrimonial relationship with anybody who is so above me, who will look down on a wife as a mere housemaid. I am not money crazy" . . . Also, *"I will not be a second wife. I want to be the mistress of my own home"* She was a very beautiful lady (still very much is) and had many suitors including rich married

men who promised to build her a hospital if she would marry them. Well, she instead married her sweetheart, a young college graduate who had no money and still achieved her goal of building a hospital.

Some she said in the vernacular:

"Eni moyi wura la nta a fun", meaning, "You only sell gold to someone who appreciates its value". This she said to us girls in particular to convey to us that we were very precious and valuable, and hence to only choose men who were worthy of us and would appreciate our worth. I grew up knowing that I brought a lot to the table, and that I would be a blessing to any man who was lucky enough to have me. I therefore had to take the time to select the man who was worth receiving this "gold package". Talk about imparting self esteem in a daughter.

"Eni puro a jale", meaning, "If you lie, you will steal". She treated lying as if it were murder. She scared us to death about lying. That definitely paid off.

In her *"Ijesha"* ethnic dialect she would say, *"On on tan ra oni i rure"*, meaning, "You cannot deceive yourself and prosper". Be true to yourself. She said this when you were fooling yourself and didn't face the realities of your situation.

"Ohun ti ko lenu ki i gbon ju ni lo", meaning, "Something that doesn't have a mouth (such as an inanimate object) should not be smarter or wiser than you are." She said this when she thought you needed to utilize more wisdom in handling a particular project or putting something together.

We thought this was very mean; *"B'o o ku, o o ni i dina orun"* meaning, if you die, you will not block the gate of heaven. She said that when you wailed and cried after she punished you for wrongdoing. She pretended as if she was not affected by your crying but indeed she was, because she would wrap her hands around you later, explaining why she had to discipline you.

Another one she said in her ethnic *"Ijesha"* dialect was, *"Esun un j'Olorun lo"*, meaning, "Nothing is greater than God". She said this when you were facing some challenges and she was inviting you to kneel with her and pray together on the issue.

Whenever she would visit any of her daughters in the United States, she would always encourage us to do something for ourselves and improve ourselves in some way while she was here in order to maximize the benefit of her presence to help out and babysit.

I am truly blessed to have been raised by such a wonderful woman whom you would call an all-rounder. Beautiful, financially independent, intelligent, yet humble in all her ways. She especially did a lot to build the self esteem of all her children. Young people of today, especially teens face a lot of challenges with self-esteem, looks, peer pressure, a sense of belonging, and so on. Her encouraging spirit inspired me to pen the following words of affirmation from God's word and I pray that they will help some youth to survive and cope in the face of obstacles and challenges that frequently plague their young lives. It is entitled:

"I AM A TERRIFIC TEEN"

I am beautiful / Handsome
For I am amazingly and wonderfully made.
Psalm 39:14

I will not leave the way of the Lord

For I am being trained to live the right way.
Proverbs 22:6

I have a lot of peace
For I am allowing the Lord to be my teacher.
Isaiah 54:13

I am special and unique
And my life will show the goodness and
wonderful acts of God. 1 Peter 2:9

I will live a long, happy and peaceful life
For I will honor and obey my parents. Exodus
20:12

I will not be destroyed or suddenly cut off
For I will accept correction and follow good
advice. Proverbs 29:1

I will achieve every goal I set for myself
For I can do everything through Christ who
gives me strength. Philippians 4:13

I have a very bright future
For the Lord has great plans for my life.
Jeremiah 29:11

I will always be on top and never at the bottom

*For I will obey all the commands of the Lord
my God. Deuteronomy 28:13*

*I will keep myself pure
For this is the worship that is truly acceptable
to God. Romans 12:1*

*I will honor God and be a Daniel, a Joseph and
an Esther in my generation.*

Chapter Six

But I am All Alone

Many times you feel that you are all alone but there is still hope. Single Parenthood should not be a ticket to poverty or children who are not successful. If you find yourself in this unfortunate predicament, brace yourself up for the challenge, draw your strength from God, do your part, and watch how things turn out for you.

There is no doubt that you have an enormous task ahead of you. Sometimes I wonder how some situations in my family would actually have turned out if my husband, as the father of my children were not in the picture. It is a daunting task, to say the least, But, here we are, so, let's move on.

You may not have a lot of money to spend on your children. As a matter of fact, in most cases, you won't! And, you should let your children understand that. They won't get all the brand name items, etc. But give them your undivided love and attention. Let them know you love them unconditionally and show it. Believe me, when children are little, they appreciate the time you spend with them over and above the expensive things you buy for them. As they grow older too, they will have memories of the fun they had with you and not what brand name items you purchased for them when you could not afford them. Children are also very reasonable and understanding and will work with you. Often times we underrate their intelligence and do not give them credit for their worth.

You may need to live under very modest circumstances so you do not have to overwork yourself and not have time for your children. You may have to shop at thrift stores for you and your children. I am not suggesting to you what I have not tried either. I was not a single parent but my husband and I had to make some decisions as new immigrants in this country. We had to do some more schooling and secure licenses in order to be able to earn a good income and that took some time. In the interim, we had a family to raise. I don't know how we would have survived without the thrift stores where I would come back with two or more bags of clothing items to last us a long time and still spend under fifty dollars. The clothes go straight in the washer and after that, they are new for us! We lived on very meager means in those days but never needed to borrow money from anyone. We just learned to live below our means and we were content.

Another one of my radical suggestions in this book is that if you are a single parent with children, you may need to place some aspects of your life on hold just for a while when your children are little and you are raising them on your own. As a single parent, you will have to be extremely careful and wise if and when you begin to date. Relationships are full of complexities and need their own nurturing that the divided loyalty simply makes things even harder for your children who need your undivided attention. A lot of wisdom is needed in this area. Parenting is hard enough as it is, and, done well, it is really a fulltime job even in two-parent households. You have to be disciplined, so the children can be. Whatever you do, refrain from living with a boyfriend or girlfriend who is not the parent of your children. In a lot of cases I have seen, children have faired much better when their primary parents have not been involved in other relationships while the children were very young. Being a single parent involves a lot of sacrifice and that is why we need to do whatever is in our power to avoid the situation.

Avoid the urge to get into a relationship for wrong reasons such as convenience, wanting a parent for your child, financial help, loneliness or just needing help with the children. A relationship based on such motives will not last. Also, if you were in a prior bad relationship, allow yourself time to heal completely and emotionally and do not rush into another one. Find a support group for yourself so you can receive your own nurturing.

Above all, stay connected with God, and He will sustain you.

Chapter Seven

I Control my Financial Destiny

Most people may not believe this statement, but I believe it is one of the most factual statements you will ever hear. You determine your financial destiny based on the choices you make everyday. Joe and Jane may begin their working life the same day and on the same salary. Just based on their salaries alone with no additional income, one of them might be a millionaire after 30 years while the other is a pauper. You would have heard the statement I am sure, "it's not how much you make but how much you keep."

America is a land of opportunity, and, regardless of where you begin, your end point can be potentially high and positive. You may begin poor, but remaining poor is your choice. For a lot of people, living below poverty level in

America is inexcusable and it is like living by the riverside and washing hands with spittle. Your financial strength is largely dependent on you and the choices you make.

Whether you are age 20 or 60 reading this book, you will benefit from the principles outlined in this chapter. But, as you will find out, the principles do not originate with me. I have equipped myself with valuable resources and have tried to apply them to my own life and they have produced good results.

Most people could live comfortably but the choices we make disallow us. During my first few years in this country when I worked at menial jobs, I would frequently encounter individuals who had been at the job, earning minimum wage for many years. I wondered why they had not seized the opportunity of acquiring more education and /or better skills. I found that there were a lot of encumbrances that got in the way.

A popular scenario is a young, unmarried mother with at most a High School education, having many children, earning around minimum wage, yet riding a new car, buying costly designer shoes for her children and having her apartment equipped with all the latest electronic gadgets. Credit cards make it all possible. I am not talking fables. It is a common scenario to see the lower paid members of an organization riding the more expensive cars. Someone has said that it is only in America that you could drive a Jaguar and not have money to put gas in it!

If a young person has a child out of wedlock when the person has not finished school or had a vocation, it actually makes financial sense to desist from having more children until that person's life is better situated financially. Not having more children at that point in the person's life may mean the difference between being poor or not.

The focus of such a person's financial future should be returning to school or learning a trade. That should also not be the time for trying to live like the Joneses. It is not the time for expensive lifestyle maintained by credit cards. Using credit cards to purchase what we cannot afford simply keeps us in perpetual poverty.

It is okay to share an apartment with someone who is similarly situated so you can share costs and provide moral support for each other. Any sacrifice made in the short term yields untold dividends in the long run.

I have also learned however that some people are just ignorant and need to be educated on financial issues. A lady told me that there was a new member of her church who was earning

$1000/month, yet lived in an apartment where she paid $500, month. She said she explained to the lady that she could not do that! By the time she paid for gas, lights, telephone, etc, what would be left to feed and clothe her children? Without an explanation, the lady just didn't figure out what she was setting herself up for.

And how about the average two income families who simply live beyond their means, such as having a household expense of $200,000 on a $120,000 income? The result is living in debt perpetually, strain on the marriage and family as a whole, and never attaining true financial freedom. I have heard that most of the people filing for bankruptcy earn six figures!

How about those who know that having a career change might better their lot, but servicing the current lifestyle will not make room for what must be done.

I will share some time-tested and common sense financial principles and hope you will benefit from them.

Principle #1: Budget your money, spend less than you earn and save

Some people will say, "duh! that's pretty obvious!" Well, the truth is that many of us do not, thanks to credit cards. When we budget, we assign a function to every dollar and we get to tell our dollar what to do and where to go. We don't wonder at the end of the month where in the world all the money went. Your income will never be enough if you do not control your spending. The popular saying is, "cut your coat according to your size" but my husband's mantra is, "cut your coat *below* your size." That way, you'll have some leftover to help someone in need.

Saving and investing are not part of our culture but there is no road to financial independence that will not involve saving of some sort. There are numerous resources available on this topic and we need to avail ourselves of them. Two books that have been very valuable to me are "Total Money Makeover" by Dave Ramsey and "Get Clark Smart" by Clark Howard. We need to become financially literate and understand how money works.

Principle #2: Forget about the Joneses

Someday, you may very well live better than them. In fact, if you follow sound financial principles and counsel, you *will*. I love Dave Ramsey's famous slogan, "live like no one else, so later, you can live like no one else." I remember the years when my husband and I did what we had to do: shopping in thrift stores, buying old, pre-owned cars (well, we are yet to buy a new car, but our pre-owned cars are newer these days) and furniture, etc. Living this way enabled us to pursue our goals, which in turn served to increase our income so that we were able to meet our needs with ease.

We knew people who did not make much more than we did, but felt they could not live as frugally as we did. Going to the thrift store was unthinkable and they had to buy new cars. Living the lifestyle did not leave room or funding for career changes and self-improvement or savings. The results have been disastrous in these economic times.

Principle #3: Be content and be confident in who you are

There is nothing like contentment. Do not let anyone define you by the material things you have or do not have. Be satisfied with what you can afford and don't apologize for it. Chances are, all other things being in equal, your lot will not remain the same and it will only be a matter of time before you can actually indulge yourself and be able to afford and pay for the things you want.

Principle #4: Get out of debt and quit borrowing

It is important to know that no one ever got rich borrowing money for lifestyle. My best advice will be to desist from using credit cards altogether because the majority of people do not know how to handle them. It is possible and there are rich people who do not have or use credit cards at all.

If you feel you must have a credit card, obtain one without an annual fee and make sure you pay on time, and pay up your balance at the end of every month so as not to incur interest, which adds up quickly.

Clark Howard says if you must borrow, do so on short term, low interest, and only on items that add value to your life such as an affordable home, starting a business, or furthering an education or retraining. And, only the minimum amount needed should be borrowed.

When my husband was going to start his dental practice, he decided he did not want to borrow money to do it and he did not. The implication of that was that he was not going to have a pristine, exquisite looking office with all state of the art equipment right from the outset. That is putting delayed gratification into practice. He saved up money first, and then started with a one-room practice with refurbished equipment. As time went on, he was able to upgrade his practice, but he did not have to borrow money for it. He is also able to keep his overhead manageable because he did not necessarily go for the most expensive facility just to create appearances.

Principle #5: Choose your career wisely and don't be afraid to change if you need to

In this day and age, it is wise to look at the marketability of a career before deciding for it. There are too many people who go to college, only to come out with no job prospects. Many go back to low paying jobs for which you need no college education. Do your research and find out in what careers the jobs are at any point in time. You need a job to provide bread and butter and then you can pursue other dreams and passion that may not generate income in the short term. Sometimes, changing careers marks the beginning of financial transformation. If you feel so inclined, please do so without being discouraged. It will require a lot of sacrifice but it can be done.

Principle #6: Surround yourselves with valuable resources and actually utilize the information you gain from them

I read books on financial matters and listen to radio talk shows that give financial advice. The Internet is also available and full of information.

How about adults who have already made a mistake, did not finish school, and now have to combine school and work. You can do it. Make it a priority to pay off those credit cards and get out of that expensive apartment. Say bye-bye to buying more clothes and shoes for the time being. See if your parents will take you back but be ready to follow the rules at home. Or share an apartment with someone to cut costs. Remember delayed gratification. You'll soon be on your own again but do what you have to do to get to where you eventually want to be.

I'll leave you with what I heard Dave Ramsey say the other day, "Don't look to Washington to solve your money problems. Recovery starts with you" (September 30, Radio Announcement).

The Most Important Financial Principle

We need to understand that God owns everything and He is the one who gives us power to get wealth (Deuteronomy 8:18). Think about it: even if you had all the business acumen to accumulate wealth but had no health, could you do it?

One tenth of our earnings belongs to Him and a faithful return brings huge blessings (Leviticus 27:32; Malachi 3:10-12). We are also blessed when we give a generous and cheerful offering (2 Corinthians 9:7). God's arithmetic is totally different from ours. With us, two plus two equals four; with God, two plus two may be ten or more. He blesses us in innumerable ways and in greater measure than we can ever give to Him.

Unfortunately, the poor and less privileged will always be among us and we are commanded to care for them (Deuteronomy 15:11). Proverbs 11:24 declares, "There is that scattereth, and yet increaseth, and there is that withholdeth more than is meet, but it tendeth to poverty." We receive more as we give and if we give too much, God will return it to us since He is honest.

Following these sound biblical principles, we will never lack.

Chapter Eight

I Control my Relational Destiny

More often than not, we have a glimpse of what may be ahead for us in our relationships but we rationalize and go ahead anyway, and then *marvel* at the results. We have a personal choice to make in this matter also. I have many personal experiences of instances where I have counseled people to weigh their decisions carefully based on observable tendencies and they have ignored counsel, only to get a divorce after two years from a spouse they knew not to have married in the first place.

I once worked with a lady who had her Bachelor's degree and had plans of obtaining her Master's. She was dating a man with a High School education who worked on and off on temporary assignments. The problem was not his level of education but the fact that he had no plans to continue his education or otherwise better himself. I told my co-worker that the man's lack of motivation was going to cause problems in the future. She told me that their love would overcome every obstacle. She withdrew all her retirement savings to fund the wedding. The marriage lasted only one year. One of her complaints was that he almost made her feel guilty for having more education and making more money. The bottom line is that the telltale signs were there, but she ignored them.

A different and much better story is that of another friend who had a wedding date set but called off the wedding when she discovered that her fiancé had unresolved anger and had a tendency to be violent. It was a very hard decision to make but she faced the reality of her situation and made the right decision. Today, she is happily married to another man who loves and respects her.

I know that sometimes we are surprised after marriage and discover things we never got a wind of, but, in many cases, we are aware of the dangers of what we are getting into but go in anyway.

It is a great thing to desire to be married. However, we need to be sure we are getting married for the right reasons and also watch out for red flags. The wrong reasons below were adapted from an article by Sheri and Bob Stritof (About.com):

- Freedom from parents (i.e. rebellious of boundaries)
- To have sex
- To ease loneliness
- To be happy
- To be an adult
- Because of pregnancy. Many women have lured men into marriage by becoming pregnant. I am aware of quite a number of instances where the men were convinced that they were not compatible with the women they were involved with and were going to end the relationship but for the fact that the women became pregnant. In many of these cases, the marriages have either ended up in divorce, or are very rocky and unhappy. Don't do it! You are only postponing the evil day to a time when everything becomes more complicated
- To save or help someone
- Because you want a baby
- For money
- Because all your friends are married

- You've always wanted a fancy wedding. It's amazing how a lot of people spend all their energy into making one day beautiful while neglecting to work on and prepare for the marriage itself.
- Fear that no one else will marry you
- Feeling too old
- Need father/mother figure for children
- For immigration purposes

If the above are any of your reasons, watch out. Bear in mind that you can only force a horse to the river; you cannot make him drink water. There is no point coercing or luring someone to marry you. You will not be able to keep his or her love. My personal opinion is that men especially need to be undoubtedly in love with their wives and not someone else so it will be easier to keep their affection only on their wives. I will advise women to put their men to test and be sure they are absolutely in love with you.

There are also red flags [some of them mentioned in 'The Youth's Instructor" (Bunch 5, 6)] that must not be ignored:

- Can he/she discuss controversial issues without becoming boisterous and angry?
- Can he/she bear to have his/her faults mentioned without resentment?

- Does he/she receive advice graciously or is he/she never wrong?
- Does he/she insist on having his/her own way always?
- Is he/she stable and well balanced emotionally?
- Is he/she naturally happy, cheerful and optimistic or is he/she gloomy, morose and pessimistic?
- Is he/she cooperative in working with others?
- Is he/she responsible or lazy?
- Is he/she careful in his/her finances or is he/she a spendthrift?
- Do you quarrel often and does he/she have a violent disposition?
- Is he/she addicted to alcohol or drugs?
- Is he/she always quitting jobs and always in financial troubles?
- Is he a predator?
- Do you observe minor ethical bridges?
- Is he his mother's boy still?
- Does he/she desire to change your personality or does he/she accept who you are?
- Is he/she bossy and overbearing?
- Is he/she flirtatious with others?
- Is he/she prudent with money or does he/she expect expensive outings?

I know women who were beaten several times by their boyfriends and went on to marry these men. How do they then expect something different after marriage? One of my mother's wise reflections is that any bad trait a man (or woman) has naturally gets worse after marriage unless of course drastic, conscious effort is made against it. I also know people who got married to known drug addicts. In such instances, the individuals need to deal with the problems in their lives, instead of rolling their serious baggage into marriage.

We also need to be candid and proactive in discussing serious issues beforehand because they have the potential of causing problems in the future. Issues about children, handling money, in-laws, household chores, and religion, just to name a few may appear simple but they need to be discussed sometimes along the way.

I know a couple who got married and had no children for many years. It was later discovered that the wife had tied her tubes before marriage but did not inform her husband either before or after the marriage. On the other hand, the man desperately wanted children. Obviously the issue of children was assumed and never talked about before marriage.

There are also issues that people usually gloss over but which actually have the potential of generating problems if not dealt with. Points to ponder upon include: Do you agree in faith, beliefs and values? Are you receiving support and encouragement to pursue your dreams and fulfill your spiritual and intellectual goals? Are you able to accept each other's habits or are you secretly hoping to be able to change some of your spouse's habits one day? Those do not usually work out well if I may say. Do I recognize and accept his or her flaws and idiosyncrasies? You lower your odds for divorce if you pay attention and are selective in who you choose to marry. We avoid a lot of pitfalls by being well prepared.

It is also important to be the right person and be sure that you know the right person for you. Some characteristics of the right person below have also been adapted from an article by Sheri and Bob Stritof (About.com). The right person:

- Is someone who you like and who is your friend
- Is kind, considerate and polite
- Shares similar goals and values in life with you
- Is willing to share in the responsibilities of the home and future children
- Does not isolate you from family and friends

- Will not try to control your life but will want to share a life with you
- Will not make you feel as if you have to walk on egg shells to keep peace in your home
- Will trust you and not spy on you
- Will not be negative, selfish, unreliable, embarrassing or critical

Most importantly, pray for God's will in the matter and pay attention when he speaks to your heart.

How about those of us who are already married? How many are familiar with the requirement of having your vehicle tuned up and checked up after every so many miles? How about having to complete so many hours of CLEs yearly in order to keep certain professional licenses? How many believe in yearly physicals? Your job doesn't trust you to perform optimally without updates, classes and/or refresher courses. However, we leave our marriage, the institution that should be our most important relational support, to fend for itself, autopilot itself, and inevitably grow weeds, untended. My mom always says that marriage is like a garden. Tend and nurture it, and it is beautiful to behold. Neglect it, and it is ugly, filled with weeds.

When was the last time you and your spouse attended a marriage retreat? Men, when did you last take your wife out on a date? We need to make conscious and deliberate efforts to relive our dating years and keep our love young, alive and fun. Marriage gets too serious sometimes but we can make conscious effort to create fun. My husband and I have been attending a yearly Married Lovers' Retreat for the last seven years and it has literally transformed our marriage. We also participate in a monthly marriage enrichment group. I can truly say that we love and appreciate each other more at 26 years of marriage than we did as newly-weds. We only wish we had utilized these resources earlier in our marriage. We would have saved ourselves many a heartache.

There are tons of resources out there on the topic of marriage. Make use of them. Invest in your marriage. You'll be glad you did. Look for good programs that have presentations for married couples and try to attend these at least once a year. Also, it is a good idea to have a marriage support group among your friends, church members and so on and encourage yourselves from all the resources available to you. More often than not, a lot of marriages that have hit the rocks will still be standing today if more deliberate effort was made in nurturing the relationship.

I will share a few tips below that have helped our own marriage:

- Our joint commitment to the Lord Jesus Christ himself. It is in Him that we live and move and have our entire being. He is the one who teaches us, informs us, corrects us, transforms us and enables us. Without Him, we would not have a marriage today. It is good for couples to worship together, rather than one spouse staying home while the other one goes to church. That way, each one hears what is pertinent to him or her and where he or she needs to improve. It will be fruitless and counterproductive for one spouse to come back from church and say, "honey, the sermon was about you today!"

- We have learnt to work as a team. The word of God in Deuteronomy 32:30 has been very real in our experience—" one shall chase a thousand while two shall put ten thousand to flight . . . ." The effect of working together is exponential and it has helped us through the many challenges and storms that we have been through as a family. Our burdens have been easier to bear with the support we have given each other. It is not, "my money" but "our money" and you come to appreciate this concept when one of you loses his or her job or is temporarily unemployed—a phenomenon that is painfully becoming all too common.

- We love and serve each other in humility and look out for the best interest of each other. We strive to outdo each other in showing kindness and try not to take each other for granted. Thinking about what you can do to put a smile on your spouse's face and actually doing it goes a mighty long way!

- We are learning to accept each other, along with our different personalities, faults and failures rather than try to change each other but continuously pray that God would mold us into His perfect image and make us all that He wants us to be.

- We have learnt to leave and cleave as God instructed and place our marriage relationship above any other earthly relationship, and, to the glory of God, are best friends of each other.

- We actually pray together! I have heard that this is a rare occurrence among couples. That is Satan's design for sure. Let us remember that a couple that prays together, stays together.

Chapter Nine

I Control my Physical &
Emotional Wellbeing

Our physical and emotional wellbeing is
another area where we can and must take
personal responsibility for ourselves. While the
healthcare debate is going on in Washington
and around the nation, there is a lot that we
ourselves can do in improving our health. No
matter the paradigm our nation adopts in
handling our healthcare challenges, individuals
will only achieve lasting abundant health if
they put in their own personal effort.

Our health today is determined largely by
our lifestyle choices and the following facts and
popular counsel are common knowledge to just
about anyone in our society.

- A diet high in fats and cholesterol will increase the risk of heart disease
- Drink lots of water every day
- Increase your daily intake of fruits and vegetables
- Cut out empty and refined calories such as sugar, candy, etc
- Exercise daily or at least three times a week
- Eat foods high in fiber
- Whole grain is healthier than white refined flour
- Smoking is hazardous to your health
- Baking is healthier than frying

It is not the intent of this book to present any research results and conclusions on health issues. Books that address what we can do to improve our health abound. I am sure we are all familiar with numerous studies that have underscored and confirmed the veracity of the above statements. I don't think anyone doubts that they are true. The questing though is, "how many of them have we adopted in our lifestyle?"

It is a fact that our current healthcare system is overwhelmed and unable to adequately meet the huge demands for quality healthcare. Many are uninsured while funding for Medicaid and other government assisted programs in many states is running low and moving towards being defunded. The good news however is that major medical catastrophes may be avoided if individuals became proactive and took personal responsibility for their healthcare.

Some of us will opt for gulping down medications rather than disciplining ourselves to make certain lifestyle changes. I remember a gentleman who was diagnosed with gout a while back. His doctor advised him to stay away from seafood. He asked the doctor if he would simply give him medication for the gout so he wouldn't have to alter his eating habits.

Even when we have gone through medical intervention and our lives have been saved by heroic medical advances, the continued sustenance of our health will depend on how compliant we are with the prescribed regimen. Two people for instance may have similar medical conditions for which they take the same kinds of medications. Person A exercises daily, feeds on a healthy diet, abstains from the intake of hazardous substances and obtains adequate rest. Person B does the opposite of all of this. Who do you think will be healthier and take fewer trips to the hospital?

It is amazing what exercise and eating the right foods will accomplish in our bodies. I alluded earlier to a man, Dr. Sherman Nagel whose 90 year old birthday we celebrated a couple of years ago. He and his wife were missionaries in Nigeria in the 1950s. They both came back to Nigeria in 1982 for a crusade and medical outreach when they were aged 72 and 70 respectively. The whole auditorium screamed and jumped in disbelief as Mrs. Nagel jumped on the table and began performing gymnastics! Dr. Nagel showed us a picture of himself at age 40 with a pot belly. He told us that at age 72, he felt much better and, he and his wife enjoyed more vibrant sexual relations than they did in their forties. They were both looking slim and trim too. The only thing they did was to begin a daily exercise program and eat a healthy diet of mostly fruits, vegetables, nuts and all kinds of grains. They also adopted the vegetarian lifestyle. Today, at age 91, Dr. Nagel is strong mentally, physically and emotionally.

The Nagels' story is not unique. During their presentation, they showed the video of a man who was 103 years old and running six miles every morning! Most people who have changed their lifestyles have seen positive results in their health and some people have had their medications eliminated or reduced due to the lifestyle changes they made.

Exercise works wonders. My personal testimony is that when I exercise daily, I feel great physically and emotionally. When I don't exercise for a few days, I begin to feel body aches and pains. Getting back on my exercise regimen takes care of the aches and pains without having to use pain killers. Exercise actually does more than tone our bodies. It does something for our emotions too. Have you noticed how exercise improves your mood and gives you a positive attitude? Maybe because you are subconsciously thinking, "I am taking steps to adding quality years to my life and I am so happy!" Just a thought.

How about adequate rest? It is also common knowledge what stress will do to our health and ultimately our survival. Many of us have known or heard of people who have died of heart attacks and other stress induced ailments. What lessons do we learn from them as far as our own mortality? Do we know that if it happened to them, it could happen to us? I once worked with a lady who overworked herself. She was a single parent of one daughter and she always said she needed to work a lot so as to provide a good living for her daughter. She was always available and never said, "No" to overtime shifts. She was on her way to work one day when she collapsed and died. I am sure you have your own stories. She still did not live to take care of the daughter she was working so hard to support.

How about simply having a yearly physical? People with health insurance do not have any excuse because you only make your copayment. Many however still do not have their yearly physical examinations. Even when we don't have health insurance, many of us can save up about $200 in 12 months to pay for our annual physical but we don't. We however have no problems spending the same $200 on a pair of shoes or a handbag. A yearly physical might reveal the beginning signs of a condition that you might be able to arrest or reverse with lifestyle changes so that you may never need serious medical intervention.

A friend of ours was told by his doctor that he had a high cholesterol and some medication was prescribed for him to take. His wife suggested that they try the lifestyle change route instead. Our friend started walking every day and eliminated his favorite fried food from his diet. After two months, his cholesterol level was normal and he did not need to begin the medication at all. Some other person might not want the discipline of exercising every day and giving up a favorite food. The choice is always in our hands.

Please don't get me wrong. By the time some of us get to the doctor, we are at the point where medication has to be given immediately otherwise it may be fatal. Some walk in with such a high blood pressure that the doctor tells them it is a miracle that they are still alive or have not suffered a stroke. Some of us want to treat a serious condition with preventive measures. We always need to check with our doctors and let them decide if our condition is at a point that we can safely hold off on medication and see if the situation will resolve by other means.

And dare I suggest the unthinkable? While we are waiting on the decision that our leaders will make on our healthcare destiny and you are self employed or work with an organization that does not offer health insurance, how about exploring private insurance for yourself if you are single or your family as the case may be? If you are in good health and opt for a high deductible, the premiums are affordable and very much comparable to other things we spend our money on. After all we don't allow the cost of car insurance to prevent us from purchasing our new cars. By the way, if you ride a new car and do not have health insurance, there is something wrong with the picture. Better to buy a used car and spend the balance on health insurance premium. A lady was lamenting to me about the $800 monthly payment she makes on her new car. She is not a millionaire and doesn't make six figures. How does a regular income earner pay that every month? My little brain certainly cannot comprehend it. We should be more concerned about a body that feels good than a car that looks good.

I am well aware that some people are precluded from being able to obtain health insurance or the cost is otherwise prohibitive because of preexisting medical conditions. These are not the people I am placing this burden on. I am talking about the millions who can and should think about ways of making their health important enough to be included in their budget. After all health is wealth and nothing else matters if we are incapacitated by ill health.

The whole point of this book is that even when we do not have the rights, privileges, provisions and opportunities that we desire or think we deserve, there is still a lot in our power to individually improve our situation, notwithstanding, and in spite of what someone else has denied us.

I recently attended a health retreat where Dr. Theodore Nicholson, an Emergency Physician told us that most emergencies are actually caused by neglect of some sort. Either external neglect such as impaired drivers, stray bullets, fire and contaminated foods which we may not have control over, or, personal neglect resulting from our failure to maintain our health—something we do have control over.

Seventh day Adventists have this acronym that sums up the 8 laws of better health. It's called NEWSTART.

- N = Nutrition (consisting of a healthy diet)
- E = Exercise
- W = Water
- S = Sunlight
- T = Temperance (moderation and self control)
- A = Air (outdoor fresh air)
- R = Rest
- T = Trust in Divine Power

If we can adopt all the above in our daily routine, we will really be off to a good start and on the way to obtaining optimum health.

How about our emotional health? Do we know that harboring unforgiveness can adversely affect our health? Someone has rightfully observed, "bitterness is the pill we swallow, thinking someone else will die." We hurt ourselves when we live in bitterness. We should not give anyone that much power and control over our lives. We should rather take charge and determine to be at peace with everyone as much as lies in our power. We will be the better for it.

Chapter Ten

Our Testimony

𝕿his book will not be complete without me sharing a little bit about the sojourn of my husband and I in the United States. We moved here two years after our marriage while in our late twenties. All the principles outlined in this book have helped to shape our destiny in this wonderful land of opportunity and I pray that our testimony will encourage you.

When my husband told one of his professors that he was traveling to the United States with his wife, the professor told him basically that he was going to the land of opportunity where you could be the best that God wants you to be or the worst. A land where you could achieve your highest spiritual potential or you could wander away from God completely. It was his choice what he made of the United States.

One of our older friends also gave us a book by Dr Robert Schuller, "tough times never last, but tough people do." My husband read it throughout our plane ride from Nigeria and it was a lifesaver whenever we became discouraged.

We were doing very well in Nigeria and some would wonder why we decided to immigrate to the United States. My husband was a dentist, employed at a teaching hospital and lecturing at his alma mater dental school. He had a very promising future. I had a Master's degree in Zoology and was employed as a High School Biology teacher. I had aspirations of completing my PhD and lecturing at a University. Things didn't look bad.

The only problem was that we had been married for two years and were unable to have children. In the society we lived in, that was a problem for us, especially not knowing how long the delay was going to be or whether it was going to be a permanent problem. People advised going to the United States where everything is possible. If you need money, America is it. You need superb medical care, go to America. Need a good easy life, America offers a life of ease.

Getting to the United States of course presented a different story. We could not get into the healthcare system. We were told that because we had a pre existing condition, we had to pay insurance premiums for 12 months before being able to use any benefit. But we could not even afford the premium because we were engaged in minimum wage paying jobs. There were no HMOs (Health Maintenance Organizations) then, which provide more affordable options now. We also encountered a lot of people who were childless, not by choice but because they were not able to. We therefore quickly realized that coming to the United States was not a guarantee that we would have children of our own. We could live here forever, utilize all the medical advancement available, and not achieve our goal. We therefore had to turn everything back to God in prayer. To cut a long story short, I became pregnant about three months after we landed on this soil, without seeing a single doctor or receiving any medical treatment, and now we are parents of four wonderful children. Praise be to His Holy name!

I think the greatest thing that has worked for my husband and I is that we have worked as a team. That has definitely helped to make each of our burdens lighter.

I mentioned earlier that we both had advanced degrees before we came here. However, I became employed as a Nursing Assistant in a

Nursing home, making the minimum wage of $3.25 per hour, working 24 hours a week and going to school to become a licensed practical nurse (LPN). I worked the evening shift and, getting off the bus at 1am, I would feel so sorry for myself for what I was going through. In Nigeria, I never knew what the sky looked like at 1am because at that time, I would be cuddled up in my bed fast asleep. I was also pregnant with our much waited for child during my one year training to become an LPN. Something happened that could only be God's providence. I started having labor pains right after I took my 3rd quarter final exam and had our first daughter the next day. We had a week of vacation before starting the 4th and final quarter and I stayed home for that one week. I went right back and resumed classes with the rest of the group after the one week break because I was determined to be done with the course that year and not take a quarter off. I could not have done that without the help of my mother though who came from Nigeria to help out.

Things were very rough in those days. We could only afford a few new clothes for our baby. A friend of mine sent me some 'pass downs' from her daughter and I was very grateful. My mom was appalled that I would put used clothes on this precious child that I had waited for and told me so in no uncertain terms. She could not understand why she was able to provide me with the good things of life as a child in Nigeria but here I was in the most affluent country in the world, putting used clothes on my child. Here was *my* world however, and I had to face it as it was, with no apologies for doing what I had to do.

My first job as an LPN fetched me $7.00 per hour. It was more than twice what I was making as a Nursing Assistant. Three months later, I got another job that paid $12 per hour. I remember my husband and I excitedly falling on our knees and thanking God for this huge blessing. The only problem was that the job location was not on bus line and I was not driving. I had been trying to learn how to drive since I was in my teens but fear would not let me get behind the wheel. We even bought a $500 car that just sat in front of our apartment because I couldn't drive it. My husband would not be able to take me to work because he was commuting between Atlanta and Alabama about twice weekly—going to school in Alabama and coming back to Atlanta to work. The thought of potentially losing this precious job motivated me to perfect my parallel parking skills and obtain my driver's license two days before I started the job. Motivation and having goals certainly work wonders.

I went on to obtain an Associate degree in Nursing and became licensed as a Registered Nurse (RN). I developed an interest in Law, determined that it was what I wanted at this point in my life, and went to Law School part time while working full time as an RN. I practice Law today. In the midst of all this, we had four children. We could not have done all of it either but for my mother-in-law graciously coming to help us during those challenging years.

Following a trip to Nigeria for our first visit in January, 1994, I developed a medical condition that could potentially have caused a setback but through the help of God, I did not allow the situation to mark the end of my progress in life. It was through the situation that I went to Law School. As soon as I started working as an attorney years later, I had to reluctantly begin peritoneal dialysis treatments. I ran my treatment in my office during my lunch hour and stayed on the noisy dialysis machine through the night. I don't know how much sleep my husband got those days. I carried the dialysis fluid in my abdomen throughout the day and had the appearance of a pregnant woman when I was not. I would cheat when I had to go to church or any public gathering and not carry enough fluid. Thank God for His grace in spite of me.

I never missed work for one day due to the situation. I remember one night when I had so much discomfort that we had to call 911. I came back home from the hospital around 5:30am that morning and was at work at 8:30am against my husband's advice. Up until that time I was a temporary employee with no benefits. It was that morning that I was scheduled to be sworn in so I could begin trying cases in court, a process that would enhance my chances of securing a permanent position. Two of us were in line for one permanent position and I did not want to be at a disadvantage. I told myself if I had enough strength in me, I would go to work and I did. I give God all the glory for that. Thankfully, I got the permanent position.

I was on dialysis for about 8 months until my sister Bola graciously donated one of her kidneys to me. I stayed home for three months to recuperate after surgery and have since been going about with unexplainable strength that could only be God-given. I give God all the glory, honor and adoration for His healing and keeping power. I also thank Him for giving me a loving, selfless sister who was willing to make such a great sacrifice for me and a wonderful husband who loves me very much and has been a strong support for me throughout. Whatever it is we aim to achieve, if we are determined and seek the Lord's help, we will surely achieve it. But we have to be willing to do what it takes.

Upon our initial arrival in the United States, we contacted an American pastor, Elder C. Dunbar Henri, now of blessed memory whom we had met in Nigeria when he came for a crusade. He knew my husband was a dentist in Nigeria and asked if my husband would be comfortable doing menial jobs while he prepared for his dental board exam. My husband stated that of course, he would do any of such jobs to provide for his family. My husband cleaned bathrooms and did other janitorial jobs, painted (even though he had never done that before), mowed lawns and worked as a security guard. As stated earlier, while we lived in Atlanta, he commuted to the University of Alabama in Birmingham twice a week for a Masters in Public Health program because he got the cheapest tuition there. He would get home and head straight to his security job where he was making $4.00 an hour. I remember one time my sister-in-law came to visit us from Nigeria and was very sad at how lean my husband was. He begged her not to tell their mother that he was working as a security officer because his mother had struggled as a single parent to send him to dental school and would be upset to learn of his plight.

Our pastor friend introduced us to shopping at the thrift store. I don't know how we would have survived otherwise especially being blessed with four children within a very short period of time. My husband became the king of thrift shopping and it was a long struggle to get him out of the habit even after he could afford to shop at regular stores.

My husband took and passed his dental board exam, completed his Dental Residency programs at the Meharry Medical College in Nashville, Tennessee and Emory University in Atlanta Georgia and we moved to Maryland where he began to practice dentistry. Things got better for us financially, but my husband still had the dream of going to medical school to become a physician. We wanted to buy a house and our realtor told us that we could afford a $350,000 one. We told him that we did not want that because we had goals that we needed to achieve first. We bought a townhouse for $125,000 and were thereby able to fulfill our dreams of returning to medical and law schools respectively. Don't let today's gratification take away the more lasting opportunity that could be yours tomorrow.

My husband completed the didactic portion of his medical training in the Caribbean and returned to the United States after sixteen months for his clinical rotations. During those sixteen months in the Caribbean, he came home the last weekend of every month, worked Friday and Monday at the dental practice where he had been an associate and traveled back to the Caribbean on Tuesday. That way he was able to see his family and also make some income. Following his medical training, he was posted to Morehouse School of Medicine in Atlanta where he completed his residency in Family Medicine. He is a board certified Family Physician today and still practices dentistry. He ended up deviating from the practice of dentistry for about eight years in order to accommodate the years of schooling and residency training in Family Medicine.

We have always been candid in carrying our children along and letting them know whatever was going on. I remember when we came back to Atlanta for my husband's residency and I was still in Law School. We prepared the children for our drop in income and told them to be ready to live in an apartment even though we lived in a townhouse in Maryland. You can imagine their pleasant surprise and gratitude when we ended up with a house in Atlanta.

As I mentioned in the financial chapter of this book, career change may be a very important tool in our financial success and many of us know that. The problem though is, are we willing to do what it takes? Are we willing to make the sacrifice? Are we willing to delay our gratification? Are we willing to simplify our lifestyle, spend less and ignore the Joneses while we embark on ventures that will enhance and positively change our destiny for the long haul? It always amazes me to encounter people who consider it a priority to buy expensive clothes, cars, and homes while engaged in medium paying jobs that will not sustain such a lifestyle. People buy homes and are eager to furnish it to the maximum right away even when they cannot afford it. Why do I need to afford it when I have a credit card to use, they think.

Our decisions constantly dictate our experience and I pray that we consider the choices we make very seriously.

Chapter Eleven

The Choice that Determines our Ultimate Destiny

We all actually have a destiny of success, which has been promised us by our creator; "For I know the thoughts (plans) I have towards (for) you. A plan to prosper you, to give you a hope and a future" Jeremiah 29:11. All we need to do is partner with and cooperate with God to achieve the highest potential we are capable of.

Unfortunately, many people are derailed from their earthly destiny because they take their eyes off the mark and fail to count the cost. Men and women fall from grace to grass; from positions of honor and respect to obscurity and disgrace. From pastors and politicians, to business men and ordinary folks, Satan seems to be having a field day, destroying people's destinies.

Great men and women and even spiritual giants fall under sexual pressure, allurement of riches, power, and flattery of success. It gets more and more scary as new names come up on the news every day and you wonder if anyone can escape!

It is extremely important to be vigilant, recognizing the source of one's strength and sit down to count the cost before releasing ourselves to some temporary enjoyment. A man who is being infatuated with a woman who is not his wife needs to count the cost whether indulging in the lust is worth losing his family, reputation and influence over.

In my humble opinion however, it is impossible to achieve real, lasting and untarnished success in every sense of the word just by one's own will power. Even in the facade of success, without God, there is shallowness and emptiness inside.

When I go through my own trials and find my relief and source of strength only in God, I often wonder how I would have coped if I didn't know God as my father. Sometimes life is very unfair and gets overwhelming. We see obstacles in our path to success as much as we try. How do we cope? Where do we draw our strength from so we can actually endure and achieve our dreams and keep from falling into temptation?

There are a lot of wonderful promises in the word of God for us but how do we suppose we can claim them without us acknowledging Him as our father?

Even when we have raised our children, it is in making the right choice for themselves that they will be able to appreciate and embrace the values that have been instilled in them and fulfill their eternal destiny. How important it is then that we understand the importance of appreciating this choice and offering it to our children and other loved ones. It is the only way to show true love to our children and loved ones. Even when we cannot be with them, Jesus will be the friend who is always with them.

The choice we all have to make is accepting Jesus Christ into our lives. That is the only way our eternal destiny can be sealed. There will be no point achieving our highest success here on earth but losing our souls and not achieving our eternal destiny, that of living with Him forever. He has made all the difference in all areas of my life and I hope you will give Him the chance to make a difference in your life too. Call on Him today. Acknowledge your sin and inadequacy. Invite Him to be your savior and Lord and begin a loving relationship and partnership with Him.

You will not regret it and your life will not be the same. With Him, all things are possible.

REFERENCES

The Holy Bible

Bunch, Taylor G. "Courtship" *The Youth Instructor*. September 18, 1956

Carson, Ben & Murphey, Cecil. Gifted Hands: The Ben Carson Story. Washington, DC: Review & Herald Publishing Association, Grand Rapids, MI: Zondervan, 1990

A Quote by Winston Churchill

Dare, Enoch & Sabainah. "Christian Courtship and Marriage" Marriage and Family Life Enrichment Seminar, Ede, Nigeria. 2008

Howard Clark & Meltzer, Mark. Get Clark Smart. New York, New York: Hyperion Books 2002

Lewis, Michael. The Blind Side. New York, New York: W.W. Norton & Company, 2009

Nicholson Theodore. "Don't Let Neglect Cause Your Emergency" South Atlantic Conference Health Conditioning Retreat, Orangeburg, South Carolina. October, 2011

Odunjo, J. F. Alawiye Pimary Yoruba Course. London, England: Longman Publishing, 1970

Omartian, Stormie. The Power of a Praying Parent. Eugene, Oregon: Harvest House Publishers, 2005

Powell, Colin. "Get Motivated Seminar" Atlanta, Georgia. November 2010

Ramsey, Dave. The Total Money Makeover. Nashville, Tennessee: Thomas Nelson, 2007

Ramsey, Dave. AM 750 Atlanta Radio. September 30, 2011

Schmitt, Betsy. Sticky Situations: 365 Devotions for Kids and Families. Carol Stream, Illinois: Tyndale House Publishers, Inc. 1997

Schuller, Robert H. Tough Times Never Last, But Tough People Do! Nashville, Tennessee: Thomas Nelson, 1993

Shakespeare, William. Twelfth Night. A Quote from Act II, Scene V

Sowell, Thomas. Black Rednecks and White Liberals. New York, New York: Encounter Books, 2005

Stritof, Sheri and Bob. "Right and Wrong Reasons to get Married" "How to Know if you are Marrying the Right Person" About. com

A Quote by Henry David Thoreau

Walker, Keith A. (Writer)& Blechman, Corey (Screenplay). Free Willy Movie. Burbank, California: Warner Bros Family Entertainment, 1993